Heaven in My Heart

Expressions of Love

A GIFT FOR

_____

FROM

_____

Heaven in
My Heart

Artwork copyright © 2002 ROYAL DOULTON
Royal Doulton® is a trademark. Used under
license by DaySpring Cards, Inc.

Text copyright ©2002 DaySpring Cards, Inc.

Published by Garborg's™,
a brand of DaySpring Cards, Inc.
Siloam Springs, Arkansas

Design by Garborg Design Works

Compiled by Rhonda S. Hogan
Edited by Mary Hollingsworth

ISBN 1-58061-360-8

Printed in China

Heaven in My Heart

EXPRESSIONS OF LOVE

Heaven in My Heart

EXPRESSIONS OF LOVE

Compiled by
RHONDA HOGAN

GARBORG'S

by Garborg's

Introduction

For nearly two hundred years Royal Doulton has attracted the best craftsmen and artists in the industry, producing the highest quality bone china. Now this prestigious international brand joins with Garborg's, makers of fine gift and stationery products, in an offering that blends the unparalleled beauty of inspirational verse with the lasting inspiration of beautiful art and design.

I never knew life until I knew your love—it creates heaven within my heart and paradise all around.

Omar Kayan, adapted

Come live with me and be my Love,

And we will all the pleasures prove

The hills and valleys, dale and field,

And all the craggy mountains yield.

The Passionate

live

Shepherd

There will we sit upon the rocks

And see the shepherds feed their flocks,

By shallow rivers, to whose falls

Melodious birds sing madrigals.

Christopher Marlowe

There is nothing holier in this life of ours
than the first consciousness of love, the
first fluttering of its silken wings.

Longfellow

Love conquers

Love cannot be forced, love cannot be coaxed and teased. It comes out of Heaven, unasked and unsought.

Pearl S. Buck

all things   VIRGIL

Forever

When true love comes, that which is
counterfeit will be recognized. For someday
it will rain on the picnic, ants will sting,
mosquitoes will bite, and you will get
indigestion from the potato salad.

There will be no stars in your eyes, no sunsets on your horizon. Love will be in black and white with no piped-in music. But you will say "forever," because love is a choice you have made.

Ruth Senter

In true love it is not we who love...

but it is God in us who loves them.

Simone Weil

When love reigns, the impossible may be attained.

Indian Proverb

Love consists in this, that two Solitudes protect and touch and greet each other.

RAINER MARIA RILKE

18

Love

I love you,

Not only for what you are,

But for what I am with you.

I love you,

Not only for what

You have made of yourself,

But for what

You are making of me.

I love you

For the part of me

That you bring out;

I love you

For putting your hand

Into my heaped-up heart

And passing over

All the foolish, weak things

That you can't help

Dimly seeing there,

And for drawing out
Into the light
All the beautiful belongings
That no one else had looked
Quite far enough to find.

I love you because you

Are helping me to make

Of the lumber of my life

Not a tavern

But a temple;

Out of the works

Of my every day

Not a reproach

But a song.

Roy Croft

The Touch

'Tis the human touch in this world that counts,

The touch of your hand and mine,

Which means far more to the fainting heart

Than shelter and bread and wine;

For shelter is gone when the night is o'er,

And bread lasts only a day,

But the touch of the hand and the sound
of the voice

Sing on in the soul always.

Spencer Michael Free

My heart is ever

at your service.

SHAKESPEARE

Thus hand in hand

Through life we'll go

Through checked paths

Of joy and woe.

We have loved on earth;

May we love in heaven.

*Verse from a
Nineteenth Century calling card*

My Heart's Love

My heart is like a singing bird

Whose nest is in a watered shoot;

My heart is like an apple tree

Whose boughs are bent with thickset fruit;

My heart is like a rainbow shell

That paddles in a halcyon sea;

My heart is gladder than all these

Because my love is come to me.

Christina Rossetti

Love does not express itself only in the

secrecy of night, but unashamed,

declares itself to the world in the brightness

of day, or it is not love at all.

Love loves all the time or not at all. It does

not hide its feelings but publicly holds

hands for all the world to see.

Mary Hollingsworth

Have a heart that never hardens, and a
temper that never tires, and a touch
that never hurts.

Charles Dickens

I met in the street a very poor young man who was in love. His hat was old, his coat worn, his cloak was out at the elbows, the water passed through his shoes—and the stars shone through his soul.

Victor Hugo

A safe and a warm and a true love ours!

There's nothing on earth to compare;

No rising crescendos

Or depths of despair

But constant, deep-rooted,

And always there!

Loretta Sulk

We cannot really love anybody with whom
we never laugh.

Agnes Repplier

My lover is mine

Love is what you've been through with somebody.

James Thurber

Every enduring marriage involves an unconditional commitment to an imperfect person. *That* is true love.

Gary Smalley

and I am his.

SONG OF SOLOMON

True Love

Love isn't the tingly sensation you feel
when you hold someone's hand for the
first time. Love isn't the breath-catching
feeling you have when you know someone
thinks only of you. True, lasting love comes
after struggling together through the hard
times, remembering the good times, and
having faith that God will help you over
one more hill together.

True love is accepting yourself, with all your strengths and weaknesses and accepting the other person in the same way. Remember that God can fashion anything out of a simple lump of clay, and He can fashion a strong lasting love out of two very different individuals.

Rhonda S. Hogan

How do I love thee? Let me count the ways.

I love thee to the depth and breadth and height

My soul can reach, when feeling out of sight

For the ends of Being and ideal Grace...

I love thee with the breath,

Smiles, tears, of all my life!—and, if God choose,

I shall but love thee better after death.

Elizabeth Barrett Browning

When you love me, love my whole person,
just as I am, and not as you would like
me to be.

Leo Tolstoy

There are as many kinds of love as there are types of people. There is passionate love, and possessive love, and paternal love, and flaming infatuation, and there is love that is motivated by a need for security. The depth of our feelings can be no more or no less that the kind of people we are.

Frank W. Gray

To love is to receive a glimpse of heaven.

Karen Sunde

There is but one genuine love potion—
consideration.

Menander

Love Is of God

Beloved, let us love: love is of God;

In God alone hath love its true abode.

Beloved, let us love: for they who love,

They only, are His sons, born from

above.

Beloved, let us love: for only thus

Shall we behold the God who loveth us.

Horatius Bonar

Love is not getting but giving, not a wild dream of pleasure and a madness of desire—oh, no, love is not that, it is goodness and honor, and peace and pure living.

Yes, love is that. And it is the best thing
in the world. And the thing that lives
the longest.

Henry Van Dyke

The Beauty

There is beauty in the forest
When the trees are green and fair,
There is beauty in the meadow
When the wildflowers scent the air.

of Love

There is beauty in the sunlight
And the soft blue beams above.
Oh, the world is full of beauty
When the heart is full of love.

You will find, as you look back upon
your life, that the moments that stand
out, the moments when you really
lived, are the moments when you have
done things in a spirit of love.

Henry Drummond

Our love is a durable fire,

Ever burning, never sick,

never old, never dead,

From itself never turning.

Sir Walter Raleigh

Many waters cannot quench love,

neither can the floods drown it.

Song of Solomon

a durable fire

Love's Philosophy

The fountains mingle with the river,

And the rivers with the ocean,

The winds of heaven mix forever

With a sweet emotion;

Nothing in the world is single;

All things by a law divine

In one another's being mingle—

Why not I with thine?

See the mountains kiss high heaven,

And the waves clasp one another;

No sister flower would be forgiven

If it disdained its brother;

And the sunlight clasps the earth,

And the moonbeams kiss the sea,

What are all these kissings worth,

If thou kiss not me?

Percy Bysshe Shelley

Love is what makes
middle of a bench

What's so remarkable about love at first sight? It's when people have been looking at each other for years that love becomes remarkable.

two people sit in the

when there's plenty of

room at both ends.

The Night has a

The night has a thousand eyes,

And the day but one;

Yet the light of the bright world dies

With the dying of the sun.

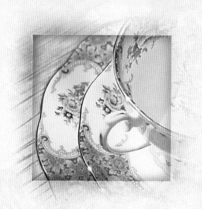

Thousand Eyes

The mind has a thousand eyes,

And the heart but one;

Yet the light of a whole life dies

When love is gone.

Francis William Bourdillon

In an old blue bus that was bumping along a dusty, back road, an elderly man sat holding a bunch of yellow daisies. Across the aisle was a little girl whose dark eyes came back again and again to the pretty flowers. The time came for the man to get off. Impulsively he thrust the daisies into the girl's lap.

"I can see you love the flowers," he explained, "and I think my wife would like for you to have them. I'll tell her I gave them to you." The little girl smiled and accepted the flowers. Then she watched the old man slowly get off the bus and walk quietly through the gate of a small, country cemetery.

Rhonda S. Hogan

Love, like the creeping vine, withers if it has nothing to embrace.

NISUMI

My true-love hath my heart, and I have his,
By just exchange one for the other given:
I hold his dear, and mine he cannot miss,
There never was a bargain better driven:
My true-love hath my heart, and I have his.

His heart in me keeps him and me in one,

My heart in him his thoughts

   and senses guides:

He loves my heart, for once it was his own,

I cherish his because in me it bides:

My true-love hath my heart, and I have his.

Sir Philip Sidney

What does love look like? It has hands to help others, feet to hasten to the poor and needy, eyes to see misery and want, ears to hear the sighs and sorrows of men. That is what love looks like.

Augustine

*Loving you and
is to feel the sun*

being loved by you from both sides.

Rhonda S. Hogan

Love is all we
that each can

have, the only way
help the others.

EURIPIDES

If I can stop one Heart from breaking
I shall not live in vain
If I can ease one Life the Aching
Or cool one Pain,
Or help one fainting Robin
Unto his nest again,
I shall not live in Vain.

Emily Dickinson

73

Love is a short word, but it
contains all: It means the body,
the soul, the life, the entire being.
We feel it as we feel the warmth of
the blood, we breathe it as we
breathe the air, we carry it in
ourselves as we carry our thoughts.

Nothing more exists for us. It is
not a word; it is an inexpressible
state indicated by four letters.

Guy de Maupassant

Trying to find yourself
within yourself is like
peeling the layers off an
onion. When you finish
you have nothing but a
pile of peelings.

Because You

Because you love me, I have found

New joys that were not mine before;

New stars have lightened up my sky

With glories growing more and more.

Love Me

Because you love me, I can rise
To the heights of fame and realms of power;
Because you love me, I may learn
The highest use of every hour.

Because you love me, I can choose

To look through your dear eyes and see

Beyond the beauty of the Now

Far onward to Eternity.

Because you love me, I can wait

With perfect patience well possessed;

Because you love me, all my life

Is circled with unquestioned rest;

Yes, even Life and even Death

Is all unquestioned and all blest.

Paul Laurence Dunbar

Love is patient; love is kind.

It does not envy, it does not boast, it is
not proud.

It is not rude, it is not self-seeking,

it is not easily angered, it keeps no record
of wrongs.

Love does not delight in evil but rejoices
with the truth.
It always protects, always trusts, always
hopes, always perseveres.
Love never fails.

The First Book of Corinthians

All, everything that
I understand

The only way to find yourself is to go
outside of yourself and love another.

Rhonda S. Hogan

I understand,

only because I love.

TOLSTOY

Two souls with
but a single
thought,

Two hearts that
beat as one.

BELLINGHAUSEN

Love Planted

Love planted a rose,

And the world turned sweet,

Where the wheatfield blows

Love planted a rose.

a Rose

Up the mill-wheel's prose

Ran a music beat.

Love planted a rose,

And the world turned sweet.

Katharine Lee Bates

LETTER FROM JOHN ADAMS TO ABIGAIL SMITH,

ONE MONTH BEFORE THEY WERE TO BE MARRIED.

Oh, my dear Girl, I thank Heaven that another fortnight will restore you to me—after so long a separation. My soul and body have both been thrown into disorder, by your absence, and a month or two more would make me the most insufferable cynic in the world.

I see nothing but faults, follies, frailties, and defects in anybody lately. People have lost all their good properties or I my justice or discernment.

But you who have always softened and
warmed my heart, shall restore my
benevolence as well as my health and
tranquillity of mind. You shall polish and
refine my sentiments of life and manners,

banish all the unsocial and ill-natured

particles in my composition, and form me

to that happy temper that can reconcile a

quick discernment with a perfect candor.

Believe me, now and ever your faithful.

J. Adams

I am your servant! Everything I have is yours. But even as I say that, I know you are serving me more than I am serving you.

At your command all the resources of
heaven and earth are at my disposal,
and even the angels help me.

Thomas à Kempis

Heaven comes
down to touch
us when we find
ourselves safe in
the heart of
another.